MW01028583

4⁰⁰

CSU Poetry Series XXXV

The Sioux Dog Dance:
shunk ah weh

poems by Red Hawk

'Hawk Fecit'

Cleveland State University Poetry Center

Acknowledgments

Grateful acknowledgment is made to the following publications, in which some of these poems first appeared:

THE ATLANTIC: "What the Old Cheyenne Women at Sand Creek Knew"; "Words are Not Actions"

THE NEW YORK QUARTERLY: "The Sioux Dog Dance" (winner, Madeline Sadin Award, best poem, *NYQ* No. 42); "How the Athabascan Hunts Bear"; "The Star-Drillers' Attention"

THE SUN: "Old Midwife, Delivering"

This book was completed with the generous assistance of an Outstanding Achievement Grant from the Arkansas Arts Council.

Cover art: "Wolf Robe's Dream" by Gary Simmons, Hot Springs, Arkansas.

ISBN 0-914946-90-0

Library of Congress Catalog Card Number: 91-71418

Funded Through
Ohio Arts Council

727 *East Main Street*
Columbus, Ohio 43205-1796
(614) 466-2613

Contents

for my dear ones:
Little Wind and Rain Drop;
Mr. J, Mr. Lee;
Dusty, Barb Bishop and Chandrika;
Mary Louise;
for my dearly beloved Osho.

Prologue: The Sioux Dog Dance: shunk ah weh

The Sioux Dog Dance: shunk ah weh

They came from Washington by special train,
generals, senators, their wives and mistresses
to see how the reservation had civilized the Sioux.

The Sioux made a new dance for the occasion.

The day was so hot flies died in the dust
and the women in lace, men in starched collars
suffered the moment their train ride ended

but they were in the fort's reviewing stand   talking
when the big drum started   on the parade ground.
They were pleased by the wooden cross they spied

in the center of the field; then the 2 leaders came,
the Medicine man and his woman, dancing naked,
holding up 2 howling dogs by their hind legs tied;

by their hind legs they hung them from the cross;
all talking ceased at once   and there was just
the drumming and the flies buzzing in the dust.

From her hair she pulled a knife and in one sweep
sliced the first dog from tail to tongue,
then passed the knife; he did the same.

Women on the stand fainted dead away,
senators retched as the bowels tumbled out.
The generals froze in their chairs, wide-eyed.

She pulled and sliced the organs into strips;
he took one in his teeth,
swung his head from side to side

and there was in that hot place

9

the slap   slap   slap
the 7 naked drummers on the big drum drumming
and the black flies buzzing as they died.

2 lines of naked dancers spun onto the field,
one by one approached the leaders,
with their teeth received the strips, replied

to the drum by howling, crouching, leaping,
slapped the strips around their heads
until they all had taken and the blood dried

on their faces. Then they ate them
one by one, the leaders going last
and on the stand there was no place to hide,

no one made the slightest move to leave
as the dancers circled and sat down:
2 old women step-danced then, cried

in a high scream   aieeee ip
and cut the ears from the hanging dogs;
they step-danced in their slow and ancient pride

to the base of the review stand,
laid the 4 ears neatly in the dust,
bowed   and laid the 2 long knives beside.

The drums went silent, the dancers sighed

and the black flies buzzed there as they died.

Part I: The Awakening of Attention

The Star-Drillers' Attention

(for Little Moose)

In a dark and narrow tunnel they kneel
one behind the other
lit only by lamps on their hats,
drilling holes for dynamite.

The front man holds the 5-foot drill
with its star-shaped, tapered point.
One hand is inches from the butt.
His beam is focused on the point.
He never looks back.

The rear man swings the 12 pound hammer
with all his might.
His beam is focused on the butt.
He never looks away.

The rhythmic noise of the blows is deafening
in that small tight place so
their ears are plugged and they never speak.
Sometimes the front man will tire
and wish to rest.

He cannot yell,
he cannot turn,
so just after the hammer strikes
he places his thumb

directly over the butt
where the hammer lands.
The rear man's beam
is focused on the butt.

He never looks away.

Little Wind in Her Joy

At ten she is ancient and still,
sits alone on the porch
and watches the red moth
struggling in a web.
When the dark spider comes
the red wings flutter loud;
she kneels close,
makes no move to interfere.
Sunlight falls
and the red wing burns low, flickers
and goes out;
still she sits and watches.

Death will stalk the hunter and the prey,
will cast its web of dark across the day,
but will not catch the silent one
who sits and watches moon and sun
as they are born and then are borne away.

The Old Woman Teaches the Young Girl About Her Body

Grandmother, my breasts are so small,
she said as they sat in the hot spring.
The old woman said nothing at all
for a long time, just sat staring
at the trees through the rising steam.
The long quiet made it seem
she had not heard; she had of course.
Then she turned. These are not a source
of strength, she said with a touch
to the young girl's budding breast,
unless your heart is free
of desire, depends on no one. Such
a clear heart is a place of rest,
a source of strength and loving harmony.
The heart of a free woman is the force
behind her beauty. Only remorse
will come to her who is in thrall
to fair face or full breast; she feels the sting
of time, old age is a gall.
But the free woman will sing
as old age beauties her and fills her heart;
her love will never fail her or depart,
not when death makes its claim on face and breast,
not when sun falls and Earth comes to its rest.

The Time Comes When It Is Easier to Die

We have to go deeper inside like
a tired miner chipping through stone;
we have to dig even when we have had enough
and it is no longer worth it to get up
out of the bed: the morning is cold,
the gray clouds move in low like a
flock of dark crows over a picked field.

That is when we have to go deeper,
through another hard layer of pain.
You have to be relentless to make it
in this place because it will be
relentless with you, it will
never stop
beating and grinding, wearing you
down with one more thing gone wrong:

friends will die or their nerves will fail;
women will cease to be thrilled with you and
your sorry efforts to hold it all together will
come to nothing; you will still tremble in the
leg, go gray and dim in the face, leak
more every year in your yellowed shorts.

Don't be in a hurry to pack it in. The
time will come when it is easier to die
than to dig. The trick is to find the
gold before death finds you and then to
sit there in the heart where you cannot
be taken while death storms and rages
all around you, stealing everything in sight
but only left holding a bag full of bones.

My Master in Chains

Tonight I am thinking of my Master
in chains flanked by 2 beefy feds
in trench coats. You have to understand
this world holds nothing for him, nothing
takes root in him, nothing
has a hold on him. He doesn't owe
a dime to this world. No, it's not him
I think of so much, it is the 2

red faced g-men on either side
whose souls are in hock to politicians;
the devil in a bad mood would be kinder.
There they stand next to something
not from this world, something
real like the sun blazing away
in a cloudless blue sky. On either
side of Jesus hung a thief; he was

lucky. The g-men are pissed off.
They had a bottle of gin and 2 blondes
from the hotel bar, high priced whores
and they could put it on the expense sheet,
call it "undercover informants." Then they
get the call: pick up the holy man,
get him to the jailhouse before dark.
The whores left and they are really rough

with the bearded man in robes. But
the one on the right is shook because he
has been cuffed to killers and cons, the worst
crazies and he has walked beside presidents
and heads of state, so he thought he had seen it all
until he caught sight of the holy man's
eyes and he knew right away he had

never seen anything like that.
They wounded and scared him worse
than a good woman's, and the hurt would
not let up so he yanked at the chains
and when the old man stumbled he
felt better for a moment. When a man
comes face to face with something like that
1 of 2 things happens: either he is ruined

for life, wanders from place to place
utterly broken and wasted so he can never
rest again; or he goes and finds the 2 whores
and when he has had enough gin he slams
into them hard so they moan and cry out and
when he gets home he slaps the wife for no reason,
working off the pain of a failed empty life
like a tired bum working off a cheap drunk.

Madness

The first to go was 2-Crows by drink.
Afraid and angry, when drunk
he pees all over himself
and rides his shaky bicycle everywhere,
constantly falling over and picking
himself back up again.

Jaynor, also afraid, went quietly.
He comes over and talks, then
just sits there, waits to be fed,
waits desperately for love to happen.
He wants to be a stand-up comic.
Once I saw him booed and heckled viciously
off the stage after 2 minutes of material
so awful it had me screaming with laughter.

Then there's me.
I teach in a hell-hole to an audience
angrier than the comic's worst nightmare.
I hold my temper, pay attention to my
madness and when I get afraid I
meditate and eat lots of sweets,
try not to hurt anyone else.

When it gets too bad I remember Jaynor
standing there on the stage doing his material,
holding on for 2 minutes in hell;
I remember 2-Crows
riding a crooked block,
falling over, getting back
on, riding, falling,
getting back
on again.

3 Gentlemen from Hell

3 gentlemen from hell arrive
at my door. They are looking
for poets to man the university
teaching positions, to conduct
seminars and workshops which
seduce the young into believing
they want to write and have a
talent to do so.

They are fat and wear 3-piece suits,
these 3 gentlemen from hell. They
have closely trimmed beards and
gold phi-beta keys dangle over the
swollen burial mounds of their
bellies. They offer small sums of
money and the possibility of tenure.
In return I must write acceptably,

poems that do not say fuck or shit,
which can be printed in journals
thick with these university poets
and their poems which not only
smell like but are full of . . . well
you know what I mean. In return,
these gentlemen offer an easy road
for art, a comfortable place to compose

dry, witless, brain dead imitations
of the witless dead in their anthologies.
They want me to beguile the young,
to lie to them and cheat their hearts
until they qualify for an MFA and can
go forth themselves, can secure tenure
and can reproduce their kind.
I invite the 3 in; we haggle over salary.

Doing Hard Time

(for Walking Eagle)

I have done hard time in the universities,
most of it in solitary, though
there were a few men and women who
comforted me there.

Now I teach all day in a harder place
to ruined children and it's funny,
some of the best teachers I've
ever met teach in this shithole for
no pay and a headache everywhere they
turn. One old boy teaches them to be
janitors. He doesn't even have a
high school diploma so
they are trying to get rid of him, though
he's the best, a Lakota Sioux who
beat throat cancer and talks in a hard
whisper like a nail dragged across a slate board

but the tough, mean little bastards he
teaches call him Pops and they love
him and they do what he says. Some
even grow up, learn respect for hard
work done well. This is what he can do,
even with no diploma, even with
no vocal chords, even with no jump on the
bastards who are out to get him.
Why is it the good ones wind up on
the run from one hard place to another,
firing their arrows until they are
used up and then,
against overwhelming firepower, they
rise from their cover empty handed,
they turn to face the well entrenched
white faced boys from good schools
and one by one they go down.

I would ponder this further with you
but they are pounding at my door.
With any luck I can slip out the back window
and make my way down the alley,
heading for another town where they don't
know me and the posters have not yet arrived.

Part II: Calling the Spirits to This World

Calling the Rain Spirit

My daughters and I once drove past a spot
where trees and grass were on fire.
We stopped: 100 degrees, no clouds,
nothing to fight the fire with.
Rain Drop was 5 then. She said she would
call the Rain Spirit   and she did.

Eyes closed she sat there
in the back seat, legs crossed
and then she fell right over.
She laid totally still.
Little Wind and I watched,
not sure what to do.

A few minutes and she sat up.
A few more and the rain came in sheets
so heavy cars pulled over and stopped.
The fire was put out at once.
I saw it happen. It was child's play.
I do not expect you to believe it;

I only tell you this because I saw
the price we have paid
in trading trust for reason.
Rain Drop knew exactly what to do
and she did it.   I saw it.
I do not expect you to believe it.

Death Don't Have No Mercy

King or bum, old or young,
when his taste is for you
and his drool is for your bones,
death will bring you down,

will drop you on the spot.
No matter that you've not yet
done what's needed, when your
lot is drawn you'll be stampeded

over the edge of a dark cliff
in a herd of weeping humans,
each bellowing,   it is not my time
and,   I have too much left to do.

I suggest when he comes for you,
friend, and stands slobbering
at your door, that you lay down
your life easily for the robber.

Let him steal your breath away and
take your frail life for his meal.
Don't dismay as your eyes go dark
and your spark of light dissolves.

He shows you no mercy unless
you show him no fear: then he
treats you to a little show, tap dances
for you and gives a sloe-eyed

yellow grin before he sharpens his tooth
and begins to gnaw at the bone. He eats
everything but the truth, so you had better
find out now what there is about you

that is true, friend
because that is what you
will be left kneeling in
when he is finished with his supper.

Old Midwife, Delivering

(for Dusty)

Her loving hands are with child;
at the end of the solitary journey
the head blooms in her gentle fingers
like a fragile seed flowering.
With silence
she delivers the race.
Her hands are the first teaching.

Then she rises.
From a small bag
she takes a stone pipe, cradles,
fills it tenderly.
She has seen many children come,
pass through her fingers like smoke,
burn brightly and die out.

She sits quietly
and smokes.

The Wheat Farmer Says Goodbye to His Only Daughter

His heart cracks like parched Earth
to see her go,
she is so dear to him.
He lacks the mirth to leap and dance,
is not free to weep,
so he walks with her this evening
out in the summer wheat
where the stalks beat softly
as his heart fills
and spills over like ripened wheat.

Suddenly his furrowed world of wheat withers
as his heart blooms;
like the last mad king of wild wheat
he grabs his child and twirls her,
whirls her through the sea of grain,
she holding tight, he boldly dancing
in the moonlight with his only chance
for joy.
When at last they fall like small toys
he is winded and amazed,
on his knees embraces her.

And then she takes her leaving
like a wild wheat flower dancing,
waving in the gentle summer wind.
He watches her go weaving,
moving slowly through the moonlight,
and he fingers ripened grain in calloused hand.
There's just one thing to do now
that his daugher is departed
and that is harvest cleanly with no waste:
in this way he pays homage
to the precious seeds he planted;
one blooms by rooting, one by blowing away.

The Old Men Go to Church

The old women march together
20 feet in front, slightly humped
as if they were dragging dead souls
into heaven.

In the wake of their chatter,
the old men are sewn in silence,
mutely suffering their spirits
to be torn from the land.

They spit, they swear softly.
They bear the preaching in a cold sweat,
but their old, wet eyes catch fire
as the young girls in the choir stand;

the old damned men are born again,
transformed by nipples hidden in thin cotton.
They stand, raise their voices for the first time,
praise and rejoice at the old desire

that lifts them higher than the Lord of Hosts.
The Holy Ghost is in their pants, not yet dead;
He makes them bold with their hands in the crowd.
He makes them pray out loud as they walk home

that they will live to praise the Lord above
and once again be left alone in that crowd
next to a pretty young girl, to brush and shove,
to jostle and jiggle their way to paradise.

The old men walk home in a riot of bad jokes;
they laugh and poke each other with their elbows.
Amazed at how the Lord has raised their spirits,
the old women march behind, quiet and glad.

Bridge of Sighs

When the river is between us
and the days drift away
like geese flying west,
I do not long for you:
I have seen how love dies
from desire,
wasting the moment
as if it were a lasting blaze
instead of a candle going out.
So I sit by the river
until the wind sighs
through the distant trees,
and then I speak your name.
If you sit by the river
you can hear me calling;
send your answer on a stone
tumbling through the clear, cold water
and I will find it early in the morning
as I go down to bathe.

When the river is between us,
I do not long for you.

Women Are Soft and Beautiful

A woman is born once,
she dies once but her freedom
is taken from her many times.

First
by her father and if he
was like mine he will
show her over and over
the pain of living, the
tragedy of beauty made to
live among the beasts.

Then
there will be the boys
later
the men but it will be
the same story: she gives
her soft and secret treasures
to their hard and hurtful ways

and when they have had their
way they will leave her in a
hurt and broken heap and only
the company of other women will
keep her from taking what is
left of her beauty and
turning it to an ugly rage.

But if she bears children in a
soft and beautiful way they will
hold her heart in their hands until
she weeps with the joy of them and
cannot resist heaping beauty upon

the dung heap of mankind so that
it blooms and softly flowers.

Such a woman dies once but is
twice-born and her freedom is a gift
freely given but never taken away.

Part III: The Offering to Power

Words Are Not Actions

I have known some,
especially in the university,
who thought that if they gave a fine talk
or wrote a long article for the journals,
this made them men of action.

The Indians knew better.
Before a warrior went into battle
he would not speak.
He would go into the sweat lodge with others;
they would drum and sing and pray.
Then for 3 days he would go into solitude,
preparing his heart for his death.
When he came out, ready to ride,
his woman would hand him axe and bow.
No word was spoken.

Some came back dead or badly wounded.
There would be a big fire; all would gather
to hear the tales of battle.
The warriors would laugh and laugh,
make jokes about each other,
tell true stories that were so and not so.
They knew the wounds would heal,
knew the dead would be fed to the birds.

The Indians had a saying:
words fall down on the ground
like shit from the dogs;
deeds rise up in the sky
like the spirit leaving the body.

The World Is Full of Experts

They are on every street corner,
on every bar stool eating beer nuts,
sweeping bank floors, cooking up
fries at the Burger Palace. They
all have it figured and are
eager to tell you the way it is and
how you are doing it all wrong.

Esther is one.
She runs the dump where I
teach. Fat and ugly, she is good
at firing people and chewing
ass. She never shows her
face, but sits in there
behind her desk and decides:
this one goes, this one
stays. She is the worst kind,
one with a little power.
When she chased my friend Eagle
this was too much for me.

I am used to the experts, they are
everywhere but when Esther
and her kind come to the gates of hell
I will be taking tickets,
I will be watching for her and
I will put her on Eagle's crew to
work her way through hell. He
will be the boss and every day
will be a thousand years.

Every move she makes will be
criticized and she will work
under constant threat of punishment
and at the end of every day they

will bring her in front of Eagle's desk
where he will sit shaking his head and
tap, tap, tapping a pencil on her file
and every day she will be fired.

The nights are a thousand years
and every night she will walk the streets
alone and unsure where to go or
what to do and on every street corner
there will be an expert standing there
and she will have to stop and listen
every time and in the morning she
will start all over again
working her way through hell
on Mister Eagle's crew.

2 Fat Women in the Bar

Their legs look like depth charges
exploded in their veins which even their stockings
cannot hide and, Oh! those stockings
with their rips and runs racing up
to the preposterous meaty thighs
they expose like innocent schoolgirls
as they hoist their beers and raucous voices.

They are so fat, these beery bimbos,
that the bar shifts and tilts dangerously
like a small, badly loaded boat in high seas.
Their thick blubberous voices careen
and crash in the smoky bar. No one
wants to look, it is too obscene,
but all eyes are furtively on them and

they know it. One rises and her gigantic breasts
bring the room to its knees. We can no longer
pretend disinterest, we scream and howl
and her red beefy face breaks through the haze,
her smile like a well-lit Halloween pumpkin,
big gaps between her spiky teeth.
Somehow she and her friend are transformed:

the mystery of women is so outraged, so
grotesquely burlesqued that every male
in the place falls in love with these sides of beef.
The riot of their flesh, the pink hams exposed
in a tunnel of torn nylon, is beautiful;
they pose no threat, no one feels the need to impress.
We all buy them drinks and they come round with

fat slobbery kisses; the bar rocks with laughter.
They dance with the drunks whose poor arms

cannot begin to contain the waddle and waltz
of that flesh: soon they are flabbed
into submission and more take their place.
They leave like bright porcine angels and every man
there feels more manly, strangely handsome,

as if for a moment they truly understood women,
knew what they wanted and knew how to please them.

Fish

No wonder they beat him
mercilessly and without ceasing;
he did not belong here
among us with a name like that:
Fish, Kenneth J., nervous tic,
stammer, jerk in his walk and in
his ways also, he
was out of his element in the Corps.

He belonged in water, not an ocean
either but some quiet bowl in an
old woman's parlor which could be
covered at night like a bird cage so
he could rest from the sorrow of
this world, from its dark and surly ways.
But no.

They threw him in here with
the land sharks who are hungry and
looking for the slightest weakness; when
they spot it they don't even bother
to circle, but go straight for the kill.
He had no chance.
But here is the thing about Fish
that finally got them all:

he took it and he
kept coming back for more. When
one of them broke his nose, they
asked him why he didn't press charges.
I felt sorry for him, Fish said and
they did not know what to do with
that. It stopped them.
They had never seen this before

and you could see it, it spooked them,
a man feeling pity for his attackers.
After that they did not know
what to do with Fish so they began
to lay off him little by little and
some even came to like him.
The thing about Fish is,
he beat them:

the nervous little jerk from a
broken home took his frail and
stammering heart in his hands
and he beat them mercifully with it
until they had enough and gave up.

Once a blazing Fisher Man came fishing here;
millions of lesser men have come along since,
but not so very many fish.

Losers Like Us

I am a loser,
one of those men for whom
the vicious meanness of the world is
more than I can bear so
I have had to shy away from it and
find a place where I can hide
and not be found out.

The world is full of people like me:
we are the ones who
gather up the refuse of the rich;
we sweep their floors and we
open their doors for them;
we are their cheap whores and
we dirty ourselves so
they can clean up.

I have seen what happens to men
like me when they grow old, how they
fish along the levee by the river near
where I stay. Every day they gather
there, shrunken inside their clothes
like vegetables wasted on the vine.
They drink wine and smoke, watching
until the sun sinks like a broken dream and
darkness covers them like a cheap overcoat.

The world has a use for losers like me.
As long as we stay quiet and make no
demands they give us an occasional worm
to bait our hook, let us bum a smoke or
give us a quarter for wine. But every so
often one of us will edge through the crowd,
step forward and
take out a politician in a quick burst

of gunfire before they can
get it together and
blow him away.
Us losers are good for that: we
rid the world of politicians and other
vermin that get in the way, and they
are glad to have us take the fall for it.

We Drink with Cupped Hands

On our knees drinking with cupped hands
from our creek
is a kind of praying
for my daughters and me.
In time of drouth
there is nothing holier
than the water in the bowl of our hands
poured over our unpraised faces
or sipped on bent knee,
giving thanks.
Religion is such a simple thing:
either it is cupping hands in deep gratitude
and filling them with creek water,
swallowing God whole
or it is nothing at all.

Beloveds, I Beg You to Be Kind

I have lost favor with my daughters
and they turn their backs on me.
They do not see yet
that their father is a little man,

not worthy of the lordly contempt
that they would give a king.
They do not see yet
that he is a good and willing target who

engages their souls in a game of chance:
he leads them far from the known path
so they might learn to love the sacred dance
of a woman who stands alone, who

does not cling to another.
She endures because
her rage and fear become silence
and solitude. Such a woman will sing

to her father as she weeds her garden,
will walk softly among her flowers and
gather her father in her arms,
carry him gently to the house,

place him in cut crystal on the table,
thank him openly as her friends sit
for dinner, and with a glad heart
catch his fragrance throughout the joyful night.

Old Man Carving Stone

He serves the stone
and the stone shapes him:
it has taught him to go slow,
to pay attention;
he has learned to be amazed.
He will hold a proper stone for days,
sitting patiently and smoking his pipe,
waiting for the stone
to reveal its form;
his hands do the rest.
He is no longer fooled
that he is the maker;
he allows the stone to use him.
In return
it shows him how to die:
patiently,
face full of sunlight,
bathed in rain, dried in wind,
slowly, slowly
wearing away.

Part IV: The Sacrifice

The World Is Full of Cowards

Once the grass on the Great Plains stood
12 feet tall and the forest stretched from
the Atlantic Ocean to the Mississippi River,
from Minnesota to Texas. The great Bison herds
were so vast that when a herd moved

they raised a dust cloud that put out the sun,
the ground shook for 50 miles like
an earthquake, and if a man stood in one spot
he saw an ocean of Bison from horizon to horizon;
and if he stayed on that spot, it was

like that for 3 nights and 3 days as
a herd moved. When they came to a river
and drank there, the water level dropped
sometimes by as much as 2 or 3 feet.
Then came the railroads carrying white men

from the east in special cars equipped with
shooting platforms on the top. When they got
to the plains, the trains stopped. Black porters
carried the long guns as the men climbed up
cheering, and fired randomly into the herds

without even bothering to aim. Drinks were served.
When they finished, the carcasses littered
the ground by the thousands. The porters were
sent to cut out only the tongues and pile them
in ice chests in a refrigerator car.

The carcasses were left to rot and
the trains moved on before the stink got bad.
In less than 40 years there were no more Buffalo.
They were replaced by a creature that roams
on 2 legs and a dim candle burns low

in the dark cave of his skull, while his heart
is a star on fire. In the shadows of the dining car,
broiled Buffalo tongue is served on bone china
by white gloved porters; he orders them about,
savors the delicate spoils. He is dressed to kill.

When death comes for the cowards it is
not nice to them: it is known to grab the
soul by the tongue and jerk it out through
the mouth, leaving it shaken and stunned
before death puts on the white gloves and

goes to work with the boning knife.

In the Alcoholic Ward

Piss smell in the floorboards.
No whiskey here.
Father has made sure;
he went on hands and knees into every room,
praying some weak-willed drunk had broken the rules.
No one had
so he drank lighter fluid and turpentine
he found in the janitor's closet.
They first let us see him a month later
after he started shock treatments.
When the head nurse wheeled him in
his eyes were as still as murder.
They still tell about the last night:
how he somehow got to the lighter fluid again
and made his way to the staff barracks;
how he beat the head nurse with her own cat
and, flushed with success,
went out by standing in her toilet,
unscrewing the overhead bulb,
and sticking his finger in the socket.

Somehow, the cat survived.

For Susan, Who Could Not Play Brahms

To truly give love you must accept death
but it is hard when you know
the way Susan went.
Her husband sold insurance
and went with other women,
so Susan started hanging out along the tracks
drinking wine with the Indians.

They still tell how
one night when she was no drunker than usual
Susan stood quietly watching the spotlight
of a fast freight;
and how she stepped calmly onto the track,
one arm raised in a casual goodbye,
and walked right into the engine.
When we went to tell her husband
he would not come to the door
lest we interrupt the Brahms he was playing.

To truly give love you must keep things in perspective
but it is hard when you know
how full the world is of insurance men
who can play Brahms,
and how few women there are
who would walk into a fast freight
for the man they love.

For My Sister, Who Is Long Gone

She was fat and mad as hell
in a way that only fat girls can be mad.
This was real trouble because
my father was a crazy drunk,
a coward who loved to beat up on
those who were small or weak.

My sister fought him straight up,
constantly. She had a crazed courage
which fat girls can get when
life has hurt them repeatedly
and they have had enough.

I respect my sister for what she did.
She stood up to a petty tyrant
and suffered tremendously for it;
she taught me the way of the sly man:
to yield, go 'round, give ground,
and with an appropriate disguise
to make it through.
I respect her for this.

But I bow down to her because
she captured the attention of a madman
and she held it skillfully for years,
taking the blows that otherwise
might have been mine,
until I made my escape.
For this I bow down to her
and give thanks.

Sakura, Sakura: Cherry Blossoms

(For Kimio Eto)

In the still pool
moonlight carves itself like a ribbon
of bright blood
feeding a dark stream.
Cherry blossoms float like a dream,
their fleshy petals riding the flood;
the soft wind stays hidden
in the leaf. The air is cool
and the maiden weeping alongside
is chilled and very
still. Today she was a child bride.
The air is heavy with cherry.

My Neighbor Explains Why the White Man
Massacred the Indians

The old man next door is a mean one
with a beautiful young daughter
whom he abuses without mercy.
He cannot stand her beauty
and every time she appears you can see
how he shrinks up inside his shirt
and his face freezes over.

Late last night out on the lawn,
they fought tooth and nail.
He broke her finger and her screams
brought neighbors and police.
Of course he is afraid of her.
He wants her too much and rages
to possess what could never be his;

he destroys what he cannot bring himself
to bow down and worship.
He promises to do better, but he cannot stop.
When he was captured, Chief Seattle said,
    The white man came to this country and
    it was so beautiful he just went crazy.
Seattle would have understood my neighbor and his daughter.

The Forests Are Far Away

We wander lost and dazed through
the endless bricks and streets of stone
and there is no tree to give us shade
from the heat or shelter us where we
can lie down under it and wait for
our death to come and take us away.

They work us to death and they
send us off to fight their dirty little wars.
I am reminded of something Gurdjieff
I think it was once said: the ants
were once a race of men who befouled,
bespoiled and betrayed the Earth,

done in by their own power;
so they were made tiny and helpless and
their task is to gather and carry away
the litter of the dead which is scattered
over the Earth profusely and will
never cease to be.

We will not be so lucky.
Our task will be to collect the endless
mountains of ant shit, grind it in
our teeth until it is a fine powder and
deposit it in vast underground caverns so
the Earth can cull it to renew Her soil.

Part V: The Dance of Power

How the Athabascan Hunts Bear

(for Little Bear)

We die by inches,
but the great Black Bear
all at once if he's lucky.
The Athabascan is a hunter.
He hunts with a long sharp spear.

When he spots a great Black Bear
he stands and waves his arms,
hollers to get the bear's attention.
He invites the charge.
You may think this is something like a matador
but it isn't.

The bull is wounded, weak;
the bear is not.
As he charges,
the Athabascan hunter drops to his knees,
digs his spear into the ground
so it is pointed right into the charge.

Then on his knees he waits,
guiding the quivering point
so the great Black Bear charges
directly onto it.

Sometimes the spear snaps
like a cheap wooden match.

When this happens, the Black Bear
does not even slow down.

The Old Blind Elephant

Once in awhile
among the young bulls,
one feels
that old Dark Eyes
can be taken.

Just one,
once in awhile,
is enough
to teach them.

The Lone Wolf

Most run with a pack,
but every once in awhile
one will run alone.

He does not long for company,
even of his own kind.
He lives at the timberline,

hunts with a watchful patience;
he waits for his opening, attacks
without hesitation when it comes.

Most bring down the sick and weak,
going for the hamstring, the easy kill.
But every so often there is one who

goes strong for the throat; you could say
he kills as much for truth as food.
He makes it plain and simple:

this is what I've got,
what have you got?
Show me.

He knows that sooner or later
he will be taken. He lives
with this truth and it frees him.

He withholds nothing, follows
only his heart, relishes every minute
because his death is so much in it.

The Gunfighter

A gunfighter is barely hidden in my artful shadow.
As I bend owlishly over a new poem, he hunches crosslegged
over the heavy smell of brass casings and mounds of powder.
His fingers as supple as a new wound, he carefully mixes

various colored powders into the cupping brass like a poet
loving his words into weapons. As he softly fits the tight lead head,
he lines bullets row upon row in front of his anxious gun
and stares at the poem on my page, his knuckles popping like shots

in the sullen room. As I revise a new poem he fingers his gun
gently under a bright light and begins to break it down,
brushing each piece with a fine horsehair brush and spreading
a thin film of oil over the tender metal until it gives whispers

of light into his still eyes. When the gun is put together
he weighs it solidly in his careful hand, closing his eyes
as he sights with his fingertips along the cylinder, his breath
shining as it smokes the polished metal. Before I go to a reading

he will stand for hours, first at the window, his fists clenching
and unclenching as he draws deep, steady breaths. Then
he will slip on tight leather gloves, tie down his holster,
and stand easily before the mirror. He will clench his fist

at his chest, drop it slowly until it is just above his gun,
and then unclench it as fast as a snake's head striking.
He never touches the gun, only nods to himself, rolls a cigarette,
and walks out into the sunlight without a word.

As I read, he has the drop on everyone. He seldom shoots;
only rarely, a line will set him off, he will move like a wolf
to people's sides, his hand will draw within a whisper of shaking,
and as I read, he will calmly blow them out of their chairs.

One for the Old Stinking Drunk

I am circling the page numbers of the
poems I like in one of his books. There
are 20 of them and I think to myself
my god how many are there who can
give you 20 good ones in one book.
I have heard all the stories about him:
how he is a puking drunk,
cruder than a street dog in heat,
all of that.
I bought the latest book by the
newest woman and there were 2
I liked well enough in it.
Now I ask you, which would you
rather have in your house: a
stinking drunk who drinks up all
your booze and pukes on your rug but
makes you laugh and laugh 20 times
in one night and gives you 20 good reasons
to be glad you are alive; or
the clean and virtuous young woman
who drones on and on and on and
if you are both lucky gives you
2 reasons not to
shoot her and then
turn the gun on yourself.

This Common Love for My Children

My love for you is vulgar, crude
as a lizard on a hot, flat stone, rude
as a loud woman in a crowded bar.
Your life has not yet journeyed far,
so you cannot know the 10,000 ways
that the strange and arrogant mind betrays
love. I won't name them; you will find
every one the way an old woman who is blind
learns every crevice, creak and secret stumble
in her well worn house. I glory in my tumble
from your childhood tower to a place
at your feet, where the dirt on my face
is soft and real, moist and cool.
It is a suitable fall for a lofty fool,
a wordmonger, a coarse braggart too proud
of his love. With age my body's bowed
but my heart's unbroken; I sweat
you through my pores, I strut and fret
you, grow hoarse and old and very still,
yet love you darlings, even when the dark chill
embraces the body and all that's left of me
is pee-stained sheets, even then the heft of me,
my belch and curse and rude fart
will rumble in the bowels of the Earth; heart
sound stops, body drops, mouth goes round
and hollow, but my love seeds the ground;
in dirt and steamy creek, in every tree
and leaf you'll see and feel it's me, it's me.
I'm free, I'm bound; on every little wind I soar,
in every rain drop down I pour.
And when your own turn comes to die,
I'll feed out line, I'll help you fly.
And when you fall like leaves, I'll turn
and rake you up in piles and watch you burn,
then race and leap upon the stack
and we'll go up like smoke and won't look back.

Tomorrow

The world stinks, people
are full of sorrow and fearful
rage. We are all left with a
hat full of rain
a heart full of pain
a hand full of dirt
a soul full of hurt and
a mouth full of worms
at the end so how is it that
people do not check out of here
right and left, just long lines
of them: pass the gun, pull
the trigger, pass the gun.

Well I will tell you why more
people don't kill themselves:
it is because of a sweet woman's
kiss, because of babies, because
of trees and rivers but
that is not the most of it;

the main reason is that we all
say to ourselves
it can't get any worse than
this, it has to get
better soon,
surely the luck will come
my way next, I have
seen others get the luck
now and then so
surely it will come my way
tomorrow.

Part VI: Returning the Spirits

What the Old Cheyenne Women at Sand Creek Knew

(Sand Creek Massacre: Nov. 28, 1864)

All along the creek bank
they crouched holding the children
until the last warrior was dead
and the soldiers turned slowly toward them
like men in a bad dream.
The old women knew what was coming.
All along the creek bank
they tore off their shawls,
their shirts, their scarves,
anything close at hand
and they covered the eyes of the children.
The old women knew that if young children
saw what men in a bad dream could do
they would not die a clean death
so they covered the eyes of the children
and made no move to run.
The old women knew it was time.
All along the creek bank
they sat with their eyes wide open
watching and rocking the swaddled children
and when the soldiers opened fire
they tumbled into the creek,
the dead children in their arms
with eyes covered
so they would not see
what men in a bad dream could do.
All along the creek bank
the old women knew how to move
from one dream to another
and take the children safely through;
the old women knew
what men in a bad dream could do.

The White Man

Let him see who really owns the land
when he slips on the rocks
and his death slaps him sideways
so his tongue lies broken
between his teeth;
let him see when he cannot rise
from the ground he owns
and the wolves tear him;
let him see when they turn
from what remains of his body,
their tongues dripping from their mouths
like cheap ribbon,
and the first summer the bones bleach;
the second they are chalk;
the third, wild grasses brush in the wind.

Let him see then.

At the Exhibition of Indian Photographs

One by one, the speakers curse the photos
for their obvious poses. They beat their chests
at the exploitation of the Indians
and the audience, stunned and guilty, agrees.

A dance team of young Indians dances.
Two old Indian men drum, chant.
On the wall hangs Brave Bull,
last of the Chippewa Medicine men.

He sits easily on his horse, tall,
staring dead into the camera, no smile.
In his arms, a beaded Medicine staff
with 7 Eagle feathers and a plain red pipe.

All the others were dead; he remained.
He wanted his children to know
what a free man looked like
so he gave his spirit to the black box,

let his Medicine show. Long after he died
generations drew courage from his face,
saw and took hold of his spirit.
He was smart. He knew what he was doing.

The speakers do not see this.
They have walked out among the audience,
accepted bows and scrapes, been fulfilled.
The 2 old drummers go to where Brave Bull hangs,

one of the young dancers with them.
They stare for a long time,
their arms around the young boy,
speaking softly. They sit down,

pull out a small stone pipe.
The young boy holds, they stuff and fire,
smoke there. They rise, take a feather
from the boy's hair, put it behind the picture.

The speakers do not see this.

Sunday Evening

Sunday is the day of the dead
for divorced men;
it is the day I take my children home.
I hold them dearly to me
with a kiss that longs for eternity,
and walk away.
Sunday is the Sabbath
and I keep it wholly
apart from living things:
it is the day of goodbyes;
the day of the dark solitude descending;
the day of the futility of kisses;
the day I stop and wave from the corner
and as the cold wind shifts south,
turn for my apartment
like a man alone in a snowy forest
turns to face oncoming wolves.

All Things Must Pass

(for George Harrison)

The angel coming through the palace window
has knocked the water vase on the sill;
it trembles,
the water shaking like timid love.

The pale, raven-haired woman sitting by the still pool
changes instantly to a Calcutta whore,
her stall infested with vermin.
She tires of knocking them from her naked sweating body.
Her bright red lips are badly bruised.

In seven years she buys her way out
and works as a porter on the road to Bombay,
forever saving her money;
her skin is lined like a parchment map.
She longs for the children in her palace.

One day she sits exhausted on a windowsill
and is instantly pale and raven-haired,
idling in her silk gown by the still pool;
she lunges to grab the vase before it topples.

The Stern Disciplinarian

He beat his wife, he beat
his daughter, he
beat me.
He beat the eggman for
looking at my mother, he
beat the cabdriver for
insulting him. One after the
other he beat up a string of
sorry losers as long as his weak
and sorry life but he could not
touch my old grandmother who
made him cower and speak with
a civil tongue. The spotlight of
her mighty glare shriveled his ardor
for punishment, made him civilized
and disciplined his hurt and
bottled rage.
She beat him
but not with fist or brawn.
So did death.
It warped and wasted him, turned
the rage in his eye to
pitiful fear, made him shit all
over himself and whimper like a
badly hurt dog run over by a car.
He trembled and begged to live.
It slapped him full in the face,
broke the vessels in his brain so
his face turned purple, ate burning
holes in his gut. Death made him
do right, made him polite and
humble, showed him who
was really boss.

You've Got to Find a Good Cover

I have been reading the lives
of the poets and there are 2
who
knew something the others had no clue
about: the one wrote
insurance and if you asked his
colleagues about his poetry they would
look at you sideways and funny, would
say, Stevens? He never wrote a
poem in his life. Hard drinker, likes
the women, but poems? Don't
make me laugh. He found a good
cover for his game;

the other one wrote
prescriptions and if you asked his
patients about his poetry they would
smile and tell you, Doc Williams is the
best sawbones in the county, he
delivered all my babies and when Jim
took bad sick and died why it was
Doc Williams stayed up 3 nights with him.
Poetry? No I don't believe I ever
saw any of it. He found a good
cover for his game.

Ah, but the rest of them: one
came from Wales, drank himself
to death; another put herself in
the oven like a Christmas turkey; a
third waved before he went off the
bridge; one was in the looney bin
so often they kept his room reserved;

one drove his son mad and
his daughter to hate; one
more and another and yet
another drank 'til they
dropped but

you get the idea, why go
on and on? Now they go mad
in the colleges and burn up in
little rooms where no sunlight
reaches them. I have seen this,
and now I understand the
other 2
who
found good cover and held
to it, never speaking of the
burning thing inside which
drove them to poetry. They

knew that if you are a poet in
this world
you had better cover your ass and
keep it hid or they will come
for you and they will eat you
alive and when they have finished
they will toss your bones aside and
look around for the next one to
come along, all the while
licking the juice from
their fingers and their
greasy lips.

Dirty Work

Bad enough the ones they got to
stab Crazy Horse
were Apache, not white; worse,
they paid them off in liquor.

Sure they were beat and starving
just like him. That's the only reason
he went, hoping that the offer of
yet another treaty would carry the
usual blankets and food with it,
enough for them to live another
week or 2. So even though
he smelled it coming, he and his woman
went anyway and when he hit the gate

they cuffed and chained him;
2 of them sidled over and stabbed
badly, with no grace or care,
until he fell like a bag of cheap trinkets
spilling out in the dirt
his last red blood. Still, he was not
ready to quit.

Somehow he raised up, grabbed the skirt
of his woman and called out into the
darkness falling all around him,
     treachery   beware   treachery
and that was the end
of Crazy Horse.

You cannot defend
against treachery and still
be vulnerable to Love so
go like Crazy Horse:
when they send

for you take your woman, friend
and hold to her skirt until
the very end;
submit gracefully to the kill
and let your blood spill
warmly in the slow
descending dark and rising chill;

and when they go
to fetch their liquor, know
that they will
be beaten and turned out. No
one likes a traitor, even
those who hire him to
do the job.

Epilogue: Releasing the Dogs

Releasing the Dogs

Some of them attack
even when I give them the raw meat.
That's why I wear the shin guards
and the heavy gloves.

Late at night I sneak over the fence,
offer the raw meat to the charge
and most stop to eat. Then I
flip them over the fence.

This stuns them. If they are far gone
they stand and wait to be recaptured;
but a lot of them, you can see it:
after a moment something wild and free

enters them; it is the wolf spirit.
They will look around.
Their nose will take the air,
then go to the ground.

With others they learn to forage and attack,
to stay hidden in daylight.
They learn quickly how to fight
for position, the laws of the pack.

From fawning bitch to ruling male,
all of them have learned who to follow.
They live and die in some wooded hollow;
they wait patiently for the humans to fail.